# ANOINTING
## *Through* FASTING

**MERCY AYORINDE**

*AuthorHouse™ UK Ltd.*
*1663 Liberty Drive*
*Bloomington, IN 47403 USA*
*www.authorhouse.co.uk*
*Phone: 0800.197.4150*

*Published by AuthorHouse 07/04/2014*

*ISBN: 978-1-4969-8516-3 (sc)*
*ISBN: 978-1-4969-8517-0 (e)*

*Unless otherwise indicated, all Scripture quotations are taken from the King James Version of*
*the Bible.*

*To get this and other Prophetess Ayorinde's Books, please visit the headquarters of World Evangelism*
*Bible Church,*

*51-53, Ogudu, Ojota, Lagos.*

*Tel: 08033055534, 08033225513, 07025883013*

# CONTENTS

BUT THE DAYS WILL COME, WHEN THE
BRIDEGROOM SHALL BE TAKEN AWAY FROM THEM,
AND THEN SHALL THEY FAST IN THOSE DAYS.

MARK 2:20

---

IS NOT THIS THE FAST THAT I HAVE CHOSEN:
TO LOOSE THE BONDS OF WICKEDNESS,
TO UNDO THE BANDS OF THE YOKE,
AND TO LET THE OPPRESSED GO FREE,
AND THAT YE BREAK EVERY YOKE?

ISAIAH 58:6 ASV

---

BEING FORTY DAYS TEMPTED OF THE DEVIL.
AND IN THOSE DAYS HE DID EAT NOTHING: AND
WHEN THEY WERE ENDED, HE AFTERWARD
HUNGERED…AND JESUS RETURNED IN
THE POWER OF THE SPIRIT INTO GALILEE:
AND THERE WENT OUT A FAME OF HIM
THROUGH ALL THE REGION ROUND ABOUT.

LUKE 4:2, 14 KJV

# DEDICATION

This book is dedicated to God Almighty, Source of divine
inspiration that leads to fruitful and profitable fasting;
He is the Giver of all grace and strength needed
to embark on this spiritual exercise.

# ACKNOWLEDGEMENT

I am highly indebted to everyone who at various stages contributed towards putting this book together. Chief among these is my darling husband and mentor, who has led me, and has lived an exemplary life in the ministry of fasting. He taught me the nitty-gritty of fasting. I am the most blessed woman on earth for being his wife!

I appreciate all our biological children for their cooperation. We shall continue to be devoted to God as we make progress on this road of destiny.

Special thanks to my sons and daughters in the Lord, indefatigable ministers of the Gospel, who laboured day and night working to make this project a reality. Know that the Lord will always be with you in power. Your reward is abundant. I truly love you all.

# FOREWORD

Prophetess Mercy Ayorinde is no stranger to miracles. She has stood by her husband as the power of God came down in many Gospel crusades organised by their ministry, and experienced first-hand what the power of God can do. The blind have seen, the lame have walked and the deaf have had their ears opened by God's power.

Prophetess Ayorinde has ministered under the anointing of the Holy Spirit to countless women called barren by the world, and has seen God open their wombs to carry babies including sets of twins and triplets. Having ministered alongside her husband in a ministry known for profusion of miracles, she is definitely qualified to share some secrets and principles that made such manifestations possible.

The vision behind this book is very straightforward: *to provide divine wisdom and instruction to every believer concerning the ministry of fasting so as to open up to them a world of possibilities in the power of the Holy Spirit.*

This is a book on fasting by someone who has practiced the ministry. She is not teaching what she has not experienced,

as she has fasted for extended periods, and have seen the results.

Many ministers are only used to the transient pleasures of food, but are total strangers to the spiritual pleasures of the ministry of fasting. Ministers today are feasting when they should be fasting.

Whether you are a mature believer with a lot of experience in Spirit-led fasting, or a baby believer with no knowledge about fasting at all, Prophetess Ayorinde has ministered in this book to all of us at our various levels. Please read this book prayerfully. Your spiritual life is about to take a new turn for the better.

PastorDeon Akintomide,

The LifeHouse Kingdom Centre,

Magodo GRA, Lagos, Nigeria.

July 2013

# INTRODUCTION

By Prophet Samson Ayorinde President, World
Evangelism Bible Church, Lagos, Nigeria.

This book in your hand has the answer you have
been looking for in order to operate in the areas
of your call in the ministry. There is a price tag
for everything worth doing in the kingdom and there
are conditions to meet. The question which the disciples
asked Jesus that day was very logical: "What is your
secret?" Jesus' answer was very clear,
"This kind goeth not but by prayer and
fasting." Matthew 17:21".

I have seen the dead being raised,
the dumb speak, the deaf hear and
mighty deliverances wrought during our
crusades in and outside the country. I
have come to realize that only those
that are willing to learn how to fast and
seek the face of God will experience
the power of God manifest in this way.
I am convinced that one of the reasons
the twentieth century church is so

> the reason
> the modern
> church is so
> power- less
> is that it has
> lost this godly
> principle
> of fasting
> and has
> succumbed
> to the sins of
> glut- tony and
> selfishness.

powerless is that it has lost this godly principle of fasting and has succumbed to the sins of gluttony and selfishness.

If the church is to see revival in these last days, like the apostle of old; if we are to pull down the kingdom of Satan and see the power of God again prevailing, then, we must learn to crucify our flesh so that God can commune with our spirit man.

Let us move step by step using the principle of fasting. May God use the pages of this inspired book to stir your soul to do what is necessary in seeking His face and finding Him.

Shalom

"Until you apply the principles of spiritual discipline, you will never touch the realm of the miraculous."
Prophet Samson Ayorinde

# MIRACLES GALORE

**T**he atmosphere was charged with expectation. We had worshipped and praised the Lord. The man of God, my anointed husband, Prophet Samson Ayorinde, had spoken the word of faith to the thousands gathered in the open air meeting.

Earlier on, a man had been led into the crusade grounds by one of his grandsons. He had been blind for some years. Medications had failed. After all hope of getting back his sight had been lost, he came down from Kaduna State to Ogun State where we were holding our outdoor programme called 'Anointing Fire Crusade, Abeokuta.' After some shouts of Halleluyah to God, he noticed that his sight was suddenly restored. His happiness knew no bounds when he ran to the platform and started shouting *alliahmdulilai* (Islamic-Arabic for praise God.)

This showed that the man was a Muslim. But when God touched him, he received his sight. Thousands of souls got converted that night as a result of that single testimony because they saw a living witness to miracles.

You see, the world will not respond to beautiful speeches made by well trained preachers in the best theological institutions. In fact, they have better speakers of their own who can motivate them. The only thing that will move the world is the manifestation of the power of God. That is what can convince the world of God's existence.

I have seen miracles. I have seen the anointing of the Holy Spirit in operation. The Lord has blessed our ministry, under the leadership of my husband, with tremendous manifestations of the Holy Ghost. But one thing people have failed to realise is that the manifestations did not come cheap. There have been tremendous sacrifices and self denial on our part.

What the servants of the Lord need in this dispensation is to be delivered from the spirit of laxity. The spirits of laziness and sluggishness have held captive even those men who started with vibrancy in them. Many have allowed strife and jealousy to dim their focus. They have abandoned the sacrificial spirit of Christ that drives His ministers to deny themselves in fasting and praying. They peddle lies, fueled by jealousy whenever they see God's power move in another ministry. They say all those who experience miracles are using demonic powers.

## THE DEAF AND DUMB HEALED

In one of the days during our Osogbo Anointing Fire Crusade, the man of God called out on those that were deaf and dumb to raise their hands. A good number of people came out alongside those that came with them. Then he asked some of them to climb up the stage.

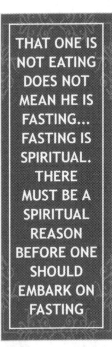

THAT ONE IS NOT EATING DOES NOT MEAN HE IS FASTING... FASTING IS SPIRITUAL. THERE MUST BE A SPIRITUAL REASON BEFORE ONE SHOULD EMBARK ON FASTING

At this point, one could feel the tension in the atmosphere as some were already saying "what if there is no miracle, what will the servant of God do? He should have allowed them to stay down on the field. See, it must be pride that has made this man to go this far," etc.

The look of anxiety was not only on the faces of the crowd;even some leaders present were already showing their doubt about the whole thing so far. Maybe because people would say they were part of the 'show' if nothing happened.

Right in front of the whole crowd, people who climbed the stage were all tested to confirm their ailment. With just one command by faith, the servant of God attended to them one after the other. To the amazement of all present on the field, they could hear and speak. Praise God!

## HUMBLE YOURSELF: FIND THE KEY

The truth is that if someone is recording a better result more than you, wisdom demands that you try to find out what are the potent ingredients he adopted that you have not. And if you are able to humble yourself, chances are that you will discover the key to the person's success and even begin to apply it in your own endeavors.

What Cain needed was not to murder Abel. He should have only searched for the right approach that made the sacrifice of his brother special and then imbibe the same.

> *And the Lord said unto Cain, why art thou wroth? And why is thy countenance fallen? If thou doest well, shalt thou not be accepted? And if thou doest not well, sin lieth at the door. And unto thee shall be his desire, and thou shall rule over him". Genesis 4:6-7.*

Heaven is full of untapped resources and only those who can forego the pleasures of the world can tap into it.

I introduce to you in this book the dimension of fasting. Ministry without the instrument of biblical fasting is weak at its best. I can tell you with the deepest assurance that one of the greatest instruments God used to launch us into a ministry of the supernatural is fasting.

## PRAYER AND FASTING: THE CONNECTION

Christians generally don't like talking about fasting. There are even preachers who go to great lengths trying to prove that Christians don't need to fast. Although many do not mind praying, if you mention anything that would stop food from getting into their stomach, they would act as if the impossible has been mentioned. And I am not talking about new believers only, but also ministers and leaders in

the body of Christ. Some of these leaders even feel that fasting should be for their 'spiritual juniors' and 'babies in the Lord'.

Fasting is often coupled with prayer in the Bible. A Christian who wishes to remain healthy must not only be interested in prayer. He must practice fasting too. Prayer is communicating with the Supreme God either by presenting our requests or It is the overflow of one's having fellowship with Him. heart towards God. Prayer is the greatest weapon that any mortal man can use. It is to commune to have a friendly dialogue with the most high.

## HINDRANCES TO PRAYER AND FASTING

**One: Sin.**

Let us make this clear from the beginning. If God must have respect for our prayer and fast, the issue of sin must be addressed. If there is a sin in one's life that is known but not confessed and forsaken, the prayers of such a person are falsehood. All should know that the prayer of someone who has an unconfessed sin in his life is an abomination to God.

> *If I regard iniquity in my heart, the lord will not hear me. Psalm 66:18*

> *The sacrifice of the wicked is an abomination unto the lord, but the prayer of the upright is his delight. Proverbs 15:8*

## Two: Disobedience

Another hindrance to prayer is disobedience to God and His will.

## Three: Unforgiveness

Also, praying to God or fasting when there is someone you have not forgiven is a fruitless exercise. It does not matter what the person has done to you, just as it does not matter whether or not the person has asked for forgiveness. If you do not forgive others, then God will hold you accountable for every sin you have committed too. If he does, where would you stand?

> *Forgive and ye shall be forgiven. Luke 6:37*

> *And when ye stand praying, forgive, if ye ought against any: that your father also which is in heaven may forgive you your trespasses. Mark 11:25*

As we move on, remove all kinds of sin, disobedience and unforgiveness so that your prayers and fasting can move smoothly to the throne of grace.

## Four: Fear

Do not let the fear of how you will look like during the fast scare you away from trying. Neither should you allow all the reports of those who tried and failed distract you from taking a chance.

That somebody died in a car accident does not indicate that driving a car is a bad thing. It only helps you to know that there are certain principles that must be observed by anyone who wants to drive and stay alive. So take the risk today and reap a trailer load of anointing for the task committed to your hands.

# FASTING: THE DISCIPLINE
# OF ABSTINENCE

Fasting is simply abstinence. It could be from food, drinks, pleasures, sex or other things. When you decide to reduce your rate of eating or you are on hunger strike, you are not fasting. That one is not eating does not mean he is fasting. He may be on hunger strike. Fasting is spiritual. One must have a spiritual reason before it is embarked upon. Certain people are good moralists. They naturally will not indulge in some things like intoxicating drink or sex. Yet this is not the same thing as fasting.

The idol and 'christopaganic' priests and prophets that are all over the place nowadays have opened 'solution centres' that the society has (even) recognised. They are not in any way connected to the Lord Jesus Christ. Many of them mix elements from both Christianity and paganism, or Christianity and Islam, and yet have noticeable results.

A closer look into their activities often shows that they possess some spiritual and mystical powers.

Nevertheless, such powers do not come cheap. They are costly. To get them, certain prices must be paid. These so called 'prophets' and 'priests' take time to pay the price. They often fast, deny themselves of many pleasures to get the power they use in their assignments.

A good example is the rain-makers. Their own job is to call on rain. In some cultures, there is the belief that if these men make demand for the rain to fall, certainly there must be showers. However, they get their powers from a class of marine spirits. To get to such a level, there are some things they must have denied themselves. Whenever they want rain to fall, they would neither eat nor drink for some days. It is during that period of abstinence with some incantations that they make their desires known to their senior boss Lucifer, also known in the Bible as the Prince of the power of the air.

## GET READY TO PAY THE PRICE

That we are Christians or church leaders does not give us less challenges. If we want to get what others do not have, we should be ready to do what others are sometimes afraid to do pay the price. Nothing good comes cheap. If it is cheap, it is not good. Original and fake products cannot cost the same amount. It is a spiritual law. If we want to become relevant in the Kingdom work in these last days, we must be ready to go the extra mile with the Lord, holding on to what we believe, even when others are turning back. Fasting with the Word and praying with the Word will give the desired result.

Fasting shows a kind of seriousness and determination that will not take no for an answer. It introduces a violent dimension to spiritual warfare.

*And from the days of John the Baptist until now the kingdom of heaven suffereth violence, and the violent take it by force. Matthew 11:12*

The place of high calling where impossibilities are turned to possibilities and testimonies is called the mountain of prayer and fasting. If you can climb it, you will surely come down with unequalled results.

## FASTING AND LEADERSHIP

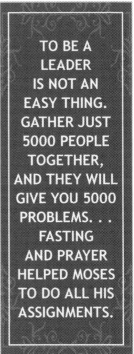

TO BE A LEADER IS NOT AN EASY THING. GATHER JUST 5000 PEOPLE TOGETHER, AND THEY WILL GIVE YOU 5000 PROBLEMS. . . FASTING AND PRAYER HELPED MOSES TO DO ALL HIS ASSIGNMENTS.

Moses' forty days and forty nights experience with the Lord on Mount Sinai could not be equaled by any prophet of his days, neither could any of them understand the mysteries behind his boldness before Pharaoh.

On another occasion when Moses was returning from the mountain where he had face to face dialogues with God, the people could not look at his face because of the radiation of God's glory that reflected from him. That was why he could lead a mixed multitude for years in the wilderness. Moses was a unique prophet and pastor with a huge crowd; he also had huge results.

To be a leader is not an easy thing. Gather just 5000 people together, and they will give you 5000 problems. So the power obtained from the fasting and prayer helped Prophet Moses to do all his assignments. Much pastoral grace is released in fasting and prayers.

FASTING MAKES YOU TO EMPTY YOUR OWN STRENGTH IN EXCHANGE FOR STRENGTH FROM THE LORD. DURING FASTING, YOU WILL RECEIVE STRATEGIES FOR THE WORK

Elijah's case was a spectacular one. He single handedly defeated and killed about 450 false prophets of Baal. He stopped the rain and did many other exploits for the Lord. At a time he fled from Jezebel a woman of great demonic power. After a retreat of fasting and prayers, he had enough power for more tasks. He returned to the same place where he had fled to complete his assignment.

The wisdom we learn from this is to know how to retreat to gather strength for the task ahead. Boldness and divine strength for the ministry comes only in fasting and prayers. Fasting makes you to empty your own strength in exchange for strength from the Lord.

During fasting, you will receive strategies for the work just as Moses received all the plans and patterns for the Tabernacle on the Mountain of Sinai. Moses' lieutenant, Joshua, and Elijah's assistant, Elisha, were people of the same experience. They were both indirectly involved with their masters during their mountain-top experiences. If Moses was not eating for forty days, it is reasonable to assume that Joshua, as a faithful and focused assistant, was probably doing the same thing. No wonder he was found fit for the task after Moses. Fasting and prayer make you focus on your projects and develop the spiritual capabilities of faithfulness to your leaders.

Elisha's consistency and commitment to Elijah paid off when the trip by divine transportation was to take the master away from the scene of history. This was just a simple example of how close Elisha was following the ministry of his master, Elijah.

## IT TAKES WILLINGNESS AND READINESS

Beloved, heaven is awaiting the willingness and readiness on our part. How much can we sacrifice for the work of the master? How far do we want to go with him? What we are actually ready to lay down for the sake of this kingdom work will determine what impact we will make in our generation.

Fasting is indeed a sacrifice and not comfort of any kind. Total sacrifice brings total results. The higher your level of meditation in the word of God, the greater your impact and result. This could be well sharpened with fasting and prayers.

# CHAPTER THREE

# DIFFERENT TYPES OF FASTING

Fasting could be of various kinds and styles. The type of fasting depends largely on what burden you have in your heart just as that of prayer depends on your desire. There are different types of fasting in the Bible, but note that God is NEVER a task master to force you to fast. It is voluntary yet a command. Jesus said "When ye fast", not "If ye fast."(Matthew 6:16). It is expected that you fast as a Christian. It is a Christian doctrine (teaching) from Master Jesus.

However, He can give you a specific instruction on how to fast. For example, I was counselling a brother in Helsinki on a trip that gave birth to our ministry, WEBIC, in Finland, a European nation close to the Nothern Pole; he needed to support his case with a marathon1 fast to make his prayers more effective but the type of job he did could not be done with marathon fasting lest he collapsed at work. As I counselled him, the Holy Spirit gave me an idea to help him. He said to me "Make him fast from 6.00PM – 6.00AM (this is a dusk to dawn fast) within which six hours must be devoted to all kinds of prayers and reading of the word for application. As I told him, he was okay with it as he closed work by 5.00p.m and resumed 5.00a.m. Another brother did his own from 4.00p.m – 4.00a.m also because of the nature of his work. What is important is to have enough time to pray during fasting. Without adequate prayer, fasting becomes ineffective.

Sometimes you need to get instructions from the Holy Spirit or through your spiritual leader who will take the instruction from the Holy Spirit. Prayer and fasting that bring results will be by the Spirit of God and spiritual guidance. God is never a task master.

## DAILY FASTING

Daily fasting could be total or partial. We also have fruit or vegetable fasting.

> "The kind as assigned them a daily ration of the best food and wine from his own kitchens . . . But Daniel made up his mind not to defile himself by eating the food and wine given to them by the king. He asked the permission to eat other things instead . . . Test us for ten days on a diet of vegetables and water . . . at the end of ten days, Daniel and his three friends looked healthier and better nourished than the young men who had day or more been eating the food assigned by the king. So after that the attendant fed them only

*with vegetables and water instead of the foods and wine" (Read Daniel 1;5-21).*

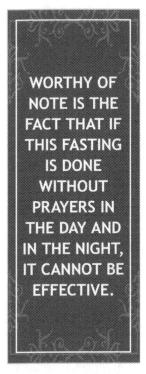

**WORTHY OF NOTE IS THE FACT THAT IF THIS FASTING IS DONE WITHOUT PRAYERS IN THE DAY AND IN THE NIGHT, IT CANNOT BE EFFECTIVE.**

When we embark on the daily fast, we set aside a whole day to seek the face of the Lord in prayers without any meal. The fast could be terminated in the evening of each day. This evening to evening is a common fast among Christians and could be for as many days as possible.

Partial fasting or fruit (vegetable) fasting is an accepted and recommended fasting among Christians especially for the aged or sickly who despite their age and health, still want to wait upon the Lord in prayers and fasting. However, some do embark on what they call 'White fasting.' This is a type of daily fast usually broken with mostly non-sumptuous foods. In breaking 'white fasts,' sumptuous foods are avoided.

Some avoid any food with salt and break their fasts very moderately.

## MARATHON FASTING

Marathon fasting could be absolute or dry. During dry fasting, water is allowed while absolute fasting means no food and no water. It is not advisable to go beyond five to seven days without food and water except by a definite divine instruction.

## THREE DAYS MARATHON FASTING

*"Go, gather together all the Jews that are present in Shushsan, and fast ye for me, and neither eat nor drink three days, night or day: I also my maidens will fast likewise; and so will I go in unto the king, which is not according to the law: and if i perish, I perish."Esther 4: 16*

In this case three days are spent in communion with the Lord in prayers and fasting without breaking (following the same principle as applied in daily fasts). The three days fast could be either absolute or dry. If absolute, one is not expected to take any food and water for the whole period it lasts. However, in dry fasting, intake of water is permitted. Worthy of note is the fact that if this fasting is done without prayers in the day and in the night, it cannot be effective.

## SEVEN OR TEN DAYS MARATHON FASTING

*And it came to pass, when I heard these words, that I sat down and wept, and mourned CERTAIN days, and fasted, and prayed before the God of heaven." Nehemiah 1: 4*

Except when necessary, it is not advisable to enter into such long period of marathon fasting. There must be a strong reason for going into such a long fast. For instance, if you are going through deliverance and there seems to be any counter attack or continuous harassment by evil spirits, you may have to enter a long period of fasting like this. Although it is the next step after the three-day marathon fast, the experience is notably different.

One very important thing to note about long fasts is the environment in which it is practised. While it is possible to do fasting or three days fasting in our usual environment, we may need a quieter place to do seven or more days. This is why many people go to prayer mountains whenever they want to embark on long fasting. The location and the environment must be relatively distraction-free to enhance greater concentration.

## FASTING FOURTEEN DAYS AND ABOVE MARATHON

*"When this vision came, I Daniel had been in mourning for three weeks. All that time I had eaten NO rich food or meat, had drunk NO wine, and had used NO fragrant oils . . . Then he said, 'don't be afraid, Daniel. Since the first day you began to pray for understanding and to HUMBLE yourself before your God, your request has been heard in heaven. I have come in answer to your prayer. But for twenty one days the spirit prince of the kingdom of Persia blocked my way . . ."* Daniel 10: 12-13

Anointing is costly. Christ was led by the Spirit into the wilderness but he returned in the power of the Holy Spirit. There is a difference between the two experiences.

*"And Jesus being full of the Holy Spirit returned from Jordan, and was led by the Spirit into the wilderness, being forty days tempted of the devil, and in those days he did eat nothing: and when they were ended, he afterward hungered . . . and Jesus returned in the power of the Spirit into Galilee: and there went out a fame of him through all the region round about." Luke 4:1-2, 14.*

Anointing for the work of redemption came fully into manifestation only after Christ paid the price of fasting and in the wilderness. Lot of Christian leaders today will tell you that you do not need to fast to get the anointing. This is not true. If Christ fasted, you cannot do otherwise.

Fasting for fourteen days and above is not a child's play. It can only be entered into only with a determined mind, by someone who has a target to reach. An unusual desire for results is what often drives men to go that far in spiritual warfare. However, it is attainable, possible and achievable. You can do it. I know people who run this kind of programme twice a year. If you see the kind of results that follow them either in ministry or life venture, as the case may be, you will know that it is worthwhile.

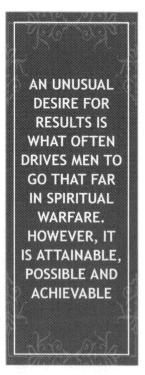

AN UNUSUAL DESIRE FOR RESULTS IS WHAT OFTEN DRIVES MEN TO GO THAT FAR IN SPIRITUAL WARFARE. HOWEVER, IT IS ATTAINABLE, POSSIBLE AND ACHIEVABLE

The target of this book is to those saints workers and wonderful servants of God who want to get into the arena of power ministry but do not know how to handle the fasting aspect of the price. Little or no attention has been given to daily fasting and three days marathon because there is always not much problem or hurdles that may want to discourage whosoever is interested in doing it. We will however explain more on the fasting experience as from seven days upward.

## THREE DAYS PRACTICAL EXPERIENCE

Use the first day to focus on prayers for forgiveness starting from your ancestors to your very self, known and unknown sins, paternal and maternal. The day may seem longer than the usual, don't look at the time, you just pray more.

On the second day, slight headache may be noticed because your body is searching for food and water all over. A voice will advise you to break and start another day may because of the headache. It is a lie of the devil. Be determined and forge ahead, as soon as you make up your mind and are determined, 'agent headache' will disappear. It is all a trial from hell or a natural reaction from your flesh. Sing hymns and worship songs and present your petition.

Congratulations! The third day has finally come, it is the final day, the day of victory. Halleluyah! All you need now is to stay quiet for instructions from the Holy Spirit. (Psalms 32:

May I say at this juncture that, there is no master when it comes to the issue of fasting. As a woman has different experiences in each of the child she gives birth to, so it is also with fasting. Each long fast you do has its own different experience and result.

## HOW TO FAST FOR SEVEN DAYS (THE PRACTICAL ASPECT)

ou can fast for three, five or seven days if you desire. A child of God who would fast should first affirm his control over food. Fasting does not kill. Those who love their belly more that God will find all sorts of excuses to avoid fasting, but those who desire the anointing would demonstrate a mastery over their passion for food. "Stomach for food, food for stomach, both will perish" 1 Corinthians 6:19. Why many of us find it difficult to fast is just because of lack of self control (Philippians 3:19). Every now and then there is always a yearning for food, drinks, sex and other pleasures. You have to desire to fast, live holy and pray.

So, to acquire something important, you must first desire it passionately, and your desire will lead you into searching it out using all available strategies. What I mean by searching is to search the scriptures to find out what the Word of God has to say about your pressing need. That is what is called desire.

As a believer, the scripture says; "What things so ever you desire, when you pray, and you believe, you shall have it." (Mark 11: 24). So, you have to know what exactly you want before you start applying solution through prayer and fasting.

"Why do you want to fast?" "To be anointed."

"Good. After receiving the anointing, what is next?"

"So that if my father is sick I can lay hand on him to get healed. Also, I must be anointed because of my child."

You can see one of the reasons people fast. Some fast so that they can see others die. Others go into long fasts for malicious reasons. In Isaiah 58,we see a good example of people fasting for the wrong reasons.

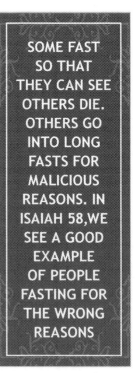

> *Look! You fast only for quarreling, and for fighting, and for hitting with wicked fists. You cannot fast as you do today and have your voice heard on high. Isaiah 58:4 ISV.*

People like this will go through the motion of fasting, including all the

SOME FAST SO THAT THEY CAN SEE OTHERS DIE. OTHERS GO INTO LONG FASTS FOR MALICIOUS REASONS. IN ISAIAH 58,WE SEE A GOOD EXAMPLE OF PEOPLE FASTING FOR THE WRONG REASONS inconveniencies, and come out of the whole experience none the better at all. They might even get themselves opened to the devil.

You must have right motive. For me I need the anointing to confirm what I am preaching and that many people will come to the Lord through me. You must look for scriptural reasons why you want to fast. Fasting does not take away the position of the Word of God. The Word must have a placement in your life. You must study and meditate on the Bible.

Jesus Christ did not wake up one day to fast for forty days just for the fun of it. At the age of twelve, he was teaching them in the synagogue. The religious leaders and the people could not withstand the level of his insight at that tender age. By the time he was thirty years old he had studied the Torah so well that he ministered with absolute authority. When he opened the book of Isaiah 61 and read; "The Spirit of the Lord is upon me, for he has anointed me . . ." He added; "this day is the scripture fulfilled in your midst." How do you think he knew it? He knew it when he was reading and studying the Torah. He knew what was written.

Can you imagine when the devil came to Jesus Christ after forty days as recorded in the book of Luke 4: 1-14? Jesus Christ did not start by speaking in tongues. It is good to pray. He replied the devil from the scripture. With that he finished him. I hope you know that Jesus did not face the devil as God's son, but as the Son of Man. He was tempted in every way just like we are. He had to overcome only by the principle of self-denial through the Holy Spirit.

## YOU WILL BE TEMPTED

Anybody who fasts for seven days should expect temptation. The devil will tempt you like he has never done before, especially the first time you do it. He will tempt you in the area of what you are asking God for. If one is asking for the anointing, the devil may bring somebody to provoke you and once you get provoked during your fasting, it will affect your focus.

If your own fasting is for prosperity, the devil will bring strange chances to you, wanting to get you involved in shady businesses. Some people have fallen into the hands of men of the underworld, mistaking Satan's trap for a blessing from God.

When you fast, be more sensitive, for the devil uses trickery and cunning. Also be expectant for your miracles because God still answers prayers.

Sometimes, Pastors are not left out in this temptation. At a time you are supposed to be focused on your fasting, there may be a distraction from a church member in one way or the other.

## SPIRITUAL PREPARATION

Make sure you are on a scriptural ground and know the reason why you are fasting. You must have the Word; you must also have a strong desire and faith. You must have love, forgiveness and cleanness of heart; hold no bitterness or grudges with anyone. Met all these requirements, then you are on a good ground and have prepared yourself for the fast.

## MENTAL PREPARATION

You must prepare your mind and continuously tell your stomach it is going on a seven-day programme. If you are married, you must tell your spouse that you are going on seven days fasting. It is not easy to fulfil your conjugal duties during fasting. For your spouse not to make demands, it is better you carry yourselves along. If it is possible let your spouse join you by doing daily. If you are living with people, they may be informed as it is necessary and for them not to think the devil is sucking your blood or that you have an illness. You may also tell trusted, Spirit-filled people you know who can pray for you also.

## PHYSICAL PREPARATION OF THE BODY

Begin to limit your eating few days before the commencement of your fasting. Start taking a lot of vegetables, fruit, and soft food to synchronize your system. It is not good to take solid meals like pounded yam on Sunday evening when you are going to start three to seven days fasting on Monday. Those that disobey this simple instruction can experience severe pain and discomfort when defeacating after the fast.

While a lot of people cannot do anything again once they start fasting, there are some however who still do their daily activities as usual. During fasting you can drive your car, travel, go to your office or go about your business. Going about your normal daily duties with good moments of prayers and meditation will prevent you from getting bored.

Some women do menstruate during fasting. This does not make their fasting unholy. Some normally feel weak when menstruating as combining it with fasting may cause dizziness; therefore take enough water and rest. Women are therefore encouraged to fast during their period. Menstruating is not unclean. It was an unclean thing in the Old Testament but the blood of Jesus has made you clean. You can have energy to do what you want to do. It all depends on the training you have given yourself. However, most of the ailments that have stayed long in the body can be healed or flushed out during long fasting.

The next thing is that you must plan your time during fasting because the devil will bring some unnecessary things to distract you, the solution is prayer. As you are making your marathon fast plan, the devil too is making marathon distraction plan. This is because he knows that for those seven days you are going to attack him. You have to be alert because he too will try to play his pranks on you. There will always be one million reasons why you think you will not be able to do the programme, but I tell you, you can do it. You can make it because you are more than a conqueror. Jesus is interceding for you.

# PLAN YOUR TIME

Then you must arrange your prayer time, you should pray for at least six hours daily and read your Bible. Two hours in the morning, two hours in the afternoon and another two hours in the evening will get you the six hours you need. Additional two hours in the night between 12.00a.m and 4.00a.m will also be adequate.

You can sometimes read Christian literature, listen to audio Bible tapes, messages and songs. Be sure you know the messages or books you digest. Read literatures that will build your faith in the areas your need. Read books that are related to your case, or listen to messages that teach on how to go along with God deeper and deeper.

"SPEAK TO ANY TEMPTING SIGHT OF FOOD SAYING, "FOOD FOR THE BELLY AND THE BELLY FOR FOOD, AND BOTH WILL LIKEWISE PERISH."

You must have plans for the duration of your fasting, so that you can be successful in your programme. One of the problems people do have during fasting is how to pray. You must be prayerful or else your fasting will be a hunger strike or a mere exercise to slim down.

You may not feel anything on the first day of your fasting but, you may be tired especially if it is your first time. Hunger will come with a lot of suggestions of 'break-now-and start-again-later' sometimes, especially during those

regular hours of your meals. To overcome this, you must be determined.

The second day, your mouth may become either tasteless or sour. This will cause a lot of saliva in your mouth b e c a u s e y o u h a v e n o t chewed food for many hours. You will smell the aroma of every food cooked around you, every orange will be very yellow and all bread will look oven fresh and hot. Meat pie will appear fresh and soft. Food will seem the only language you can understand. At this point, I would always ask myself standing in front of a mirror, which of these have I not tasted before and what miracle have they brought me, except more fat that I need to work hard to burn? Again, when I am getting lean, people or my mirror will always say you are shrinking but my reply is always I am getting FAT in the spirit. After all, no one fasts and get fatter. Then all arguments of the mind ceases. It is at this point that the Word of God should come alive in you. Remember "Man shall not live by bread alone". Always say this to yourself again and again. Speak to any tempting sight of food saying, "Food for the belly and the belly for food, and both will likewise perish." The second day is the most troublesome day.

The third day you may feel very weak. While everybody is laughing, you may get easily irritated and easily provoked. Smile and say Jesus is Lord. You may not be able to sleep well the third night. It is normal and you will also find it difficult to pray. Force yourself to pray. Ask God for inner strength.

What you will do is to get a cup of warm water and sip it slowly. As you are sipping it, strength will be coming to you. This will give you energy to pray. Because you are thirsty; you should not rush the intake of water so that you will not become too weak or even develop stomach ache. If you wake up on the fourth day you may have little stomach cramp and little headache because for three days you have not eaten.

Your mouth will have more bacteria and may smell, so if you have some antiseptic mouth wash, use it regularly. This is to avoid irritation. To some people, the use of local chewing stick is preferable. Toothpaste will not clean your mouth; you sometimes will not be able to swallow your saliva until you brush your teeth, as the irritation can cause you to have stomach upset. Drink a cup of water after brushing your teeth.

On the fifth day when you wake up, take a short walk or do a little exercise. Strength will come on the fifth day. You will probably be dizzy if you are not drinking enough water. You will feel like lying down. If you sleep too much you will have a little headache. It is not a demonic attack; it may because you are lying down too much. If you start to feel dizzy, it may mean that the liquid level in you is low. So drink enough water though slowly.

Your urine will become yellowish as if you have malaria. This is just because your system has no more food to work upon and has decided to revisit any stored up vitamins and protein in your body. Those who are naturally fat will start to lose weight.

The fifth day experience is not as tough as the fourth day. However, you must make sure that you drink enough water. This will serving two purposes. The first is that your system will have enough water to do what I will call 'house cleaning.' Then the water you are drinking is the only 'food' your body has to keep moving. Attend to your deliverance between your 5th and 6th day, if the duration of your fast is just 7days.

On the sixth day, you will almost end your fasting if you are not determined. This is because hunger will bite once in a while with all or part of your body complaining that they can no longer continue. Do not be overtaken by your feelings. Get enough rest: that is, do not do too much hard work. Drink sufficient water of about at least 6 to 8 glasses or more tha one litre daily. Pray always, getting someone to pray with at intervals like a prayer partner will help at this time.

If you are doing just seven days, the sixth day usually comes with mixed feeling. You will be saying it is just tomorrow, so one moment you will feel strong, the second moment you may feel weak and tired. The pace of time will look very slow. If you have good prayer partners you will not feel it much. You will be able to pray together.

The longest hour of your life will be the night of the seventh day. The moment you wake up you will be happy. Your mind will be settled on one fact; I am breaking this fast today; strength will return to you. You will feel fulfilled. If you want to help yourself, do not keep busy looking at the watch.

Get to prayer and read the Word of God. If your reason for fasting is related to deliverance, try and get to your pastor or counsellor before you break. You will need that last minute prayer with him.

## HOW TO BREAK SEVEN DAYS FASTING

From the noon of the seventh day you can start breaking your fast if you are stopping on seven days. It is an important point to know that; fasting is not as tough as breaking the fast. How do you break? You can break with thin pap, tea or fruits. A good advice here is that you should not break your long fast with bananas, it can block your intestine. You are also advised not to drink milk or yoghourt when breaking any long fasting.

The day you break, stay on liquid food only. It is not wise to break with solid foods such as yam, eba or rice. Do not say you have not been eating for seven days and eat pounded yam. It will disorganise your system. When people do not break properly, they have constipation and may not be able to sleep all through the night. You must break in levels. At this time, a great deal of common sense is required.

When you notice that you are having uncomfortable feelings within your system such as having a bloated tummy, continuous belching, and irritation as if you want to vomit, the next thing is to stop eating and start fasting again. This may go for the next two days before you feel better. You can now start on water only. Then be more careful or else you may need to repeat the process again if anything goes wrong.

Great care should be taken when breaking using natural fruits. Chemically preserved juices may result in your having dysentery if overused or undiluted.

After the fasting, make sure that you are in an attitude of prayer.

> Take ye heed, watch and pray: for ye know not when the time is. "Mark 13:33
>
> Watch ye and pray, lest ye enter into temptation." Mark 14:38.
>
> But thou when thou prayest enter into thy closet and when thou has shut thy door, pray to thy Father which is in secret; and thy Father which sees in secret shall reward thee openly." Matthew 6:6.

Hence, be expectant. Expect your miracle.

> *"And the people cried unto Moses; and when Moses prayed unto the lord, the fire was quenched." Numbers 11:2*
>
> *For this child I prayed; and the lord has given me my petition which I asked of him. 1 Samuel 1:27.*
>
> *The effectual fervent prayer of a righteous man avails much" James 5: 16.*

# BE CONSCIOUS OF CONFESSION. . .

*For if a man offend not in word, the same is a perfect man . . . but the tongue can do man tame; it is unruly evil, full of deadly poison. Out of the same mouth proceeds blessing and cursing. My brethren, these things ought not so to be. James 3:2, 8, 10.*

## READ YOUR BIBLE

*This book of the law shall not depart out of thy mouth; but thou shall meditate therein day and night that thou mayest observe to do according to all that is shall have good success." Joshua 1:8*

*Thy word have I hid in my heart, that I may not sin against thee" Psalm 119:11 "Study to shew thyself approved unto God, a workman that needed not to be ashamed, rightly dividing the word of truth." 2Timothy 2 :15*

Attend fellowship every time. Make sure you keep building up yourself. Do not relax. "Not forsaking the assembling of ourselves together, as the manner of some is; but exhorting one another: and so much the more, as ye the day approaching." Hebrews 10:25.

Watch your reading and make sure that the Word of God is constantly kept in your mind. If you do all these things, you will have a tremendous result.

If you are a man of God, that is, a minister that has done seven days fasting, handling deliverance of casting out demons will become easier. Some level of spiritual gifts will start to manifest in your life and ministry after seven days. If you had certain gifts before that have ceased to manifest, they will be stirred up.

*"Wherefore I put thee in remembrance that thou stir up the gift of God, which is in thee by the putting on of my hands. For God hath not given us the spirit of fear; but of power, of love and of sound mind." 2 Timothy 1:6-7*

If your own fasting is for deliverance, then you will be delivered. You will not be able to deliver yourself. Yield to a deliverance minister who will attend to you.

> *But thus saith the Lord, even the captives of the mighty shall be taken away, and the prey of the terrible shall be delivered: for I will contend with him that contendeth with thee and I will save thy children."Isaiah 49:25.*

If it is a serious deliverance, it is like somebody whose hands are tied. He will find it difficult to deliver or loose himself. It is not by power nor by might, but by the power of the Holy Spirit. He will need the help of a deliverance minister to be delivered.

May God give us the grace as we desire more of His Spirit's indwelling in us, and may all the gifts of the Spirit like discerning of the spirits, prophecy, healing, word of wisdom, word of knowledge, and others manifest in us with a greater dimension of anointing. (Amen).

# HOW TO FAST FOR
# FOURTEEN DAYS

After a seven-day marathon experience, many people often go for the next stage of fasting which is ten-day marathon fast. The experience is a little superior to that of seven days. After the seventh day of fasting, it becomes easier to enter into the spiritual realm and this therefore makes any marathon fast above seven days more interesting.

The next point of call in spiritual fasting after ten days is fourteen days. This is very close to doing ten days in some of the experiences encountered while embarking on it. Therefore, we shall concentrate on discussing the fourteen days marathon fasting experience.

The first 3 days will be for confessing all your sins, the sins of your family, the sins of the church, body of Christ if you are a man of God over an assembly, and the sins of the community. Tell God to show you every hidden sin and ask for forgiveness in the name of Jesus.

> Now when Ezra had prayed, and when he had confessed, weeping and casting himself down before the house of God, there assembled unto him out of Israel a very great congregation of men, women and children: for the people wept very sore. Ezra 10:1

> And it came to pass, when I heard these words that I sat down and wept, and mourned certain days, and fasted, and prayed before the God of heaven . . . for the children of Israel thy servants and confess the sins of the children of Israel, which we have sinned against thee: both I and my father's house have sinned." Nehemiah 1:4-6.

After 3-4 days, ask God to cleanse you and remove every impurity, and He will cleanse you.

The simple truth is that if you are able to handle seven days fasting with all the attendant pressures, then with a little push, you will be able to handle 10 to 14 days conveniently. The courage that motivated you for the first seven days is all you need to build upon. Because you are not stopping on the seventh day, you will have to contend with the same pressure that comes on the sixth and ninth day.

You may have pain in your joints, constant weakness in your body, a little headache now and then, or irritation and a little aggression. Greetings from friends and neighbours can become offensive to you. If you sit down, you will think that walking around may be better. If you are standing up, your body will tell you that lying down may be better off. Your mouth becomes heavy. You will not be able to crack any joke or laugh as usual. If you are a civil servant, it is advisable that you plan your fasting to fall on your leave period as you may not be able to do your normal duty.

Water will start to become tasteless to you. The way out is: do not drink any cold water again. If possible, heat up the water you will drink a little. Do not change your type of water intake again, i.e. drink warm water always.

If you are finding it difficult to drink even the warm water, add a teaspoon of honey and a flat level of a measure of teaspoon of milk to a measure of a glass cup of water that you want to drink.

Please be careful in doing this as you may be tempted to drink the solution directly. You are not adding the honey because you want to break. You are only changing the taste of the water. You can also change the taste of your water by adding coconut water. It is refreshing if you make it warm. In the olden days, our fathers in the Lord used 'omi ogi,' the slightly fermented liquid by-product of pap. They would warm it and sip gradually, just to change the taste of the water. This experience makes me highly respect Prophet Moses, Joshua, Elijah, Elisha and honour Master Jesus' fasting in the wilderness. No hot water, no pillow, no bed, no hymns, no complete Bible, no novels, no Christian tapes, no worship songs/tapes, etc. They did their long marathon under a harsh weather and hard conditions. Oh! They were unique!

Always make sure you stay in a well ventilated place as you will need all the freshness of the cool air that you can get. You may find out that your body temperature is always fluctuating, don't be worried. You are not feeling too hot, get to the that you can get having any fever. If you are bathroom and shower.

ALWAYS MAKE SURE YOU STAY IN A WELL VENTILATED PLACE AS YOU WILL NEED ALL THE FRESHNESS OF THE COOL AIR THAT YOU CAN GET.

Sleeping in the night may be a little difficult sometimes, so try as much as possible to take some nap during the day. You will need the sleep to help keep your body healthy. If you need to sleep much, I will suggest that your sleep should be in the day and your prayer and study should be more in the night.

The twelfth and thirteenth days are the hardest if you are stopping on the fourteenth day. It may appear as if you are going to faint. It is just a reaction from your body because you are beginning to see yourself eating in a few hours time. Your feelings are a response to hunger that is returning.

On the fourteenth day, you will be surprised about how strong your body will be when you wake up. This is just for the simple fact that you know that you have come

to the end of the programme. The responsibility of praying throughout this period of your fasting must not be underestimated. Sometimes, you will be able to pray well. Some other times, prayer will be difficult. In all, you must pray.

Note that Satan can never encourage you to fast. Why would he? He knows the result of fasting righteous living, joy in the Holy Ghost, forgiveness, rededication, focus on spiritual things, etc and cannot encourage you. So don't expect the devil to pet you or say "Well done". Instead, he will tell you so cunningly and smoothly that you have tried, assuming you are on a journey of fourteen days. When you get to the ninth day, he will make you feel you have really tried after all, you have never done it before. If you allow him in and nod your head, give him an inch, he will take a mile. He will be on you until you break. Immediately you break, he will bring condemnation and you then hate yourself for breaking the fast. So never listen to him. Matthew 4 is your perfect example. He (the devil) never leaves us alone even when we are fasting. And the good Word never leaves us too nor does He forsake us. So, whose voice will you listen to? It is a must to know the Shepherd's voice!

# BREAKING FOURTEEN-DAYS FASTS

**B**reaking a fourteen days fast must be done with extra care. Do not rush into eating. Observe all cautions. Any attempt by you to eat at the rate of how hungry you are can lead to some distortion of your body system. Stay on natural/organic juice for the first 24 hours of breaking.

If you must eat anything the day you break, it should not be more than fish 'pepper soup.' Do not eat meat. This may be too much for your digestive system to handle. Light pap or custard is good for the following morning. The use of milk could be dangerous. If you cannot drink your custard without milk, then avoid taking the custard and the custard must not be too thick.

Eating meat on the first day of breaking a seven day, ten-day or fourteen-day marathon fast can result in a serious stomach ache; the kind of pain that could be as much as that of labour pains in women. Women will understand what this is. This is the kind of pain that normally comes around the waist and below the abdomen.

So, it is wrong to eat meat while breaking a long fast. The taste of the meat is enjoyable in the mouth. Yes, you need to exercise your mouth and jaws after a long break, but will you be able to chew the meat just to exercise your mouth and then throw the meat out? It is tempting because you might end up swallowing it. This is dangerous to your system after a long break.

For example, I remember the time my husband did his first forty-day marathon. I joined him but I could only do daily fasting because I needed my stamina as a civil servant to go to work. Joining him with seven-day marathon to end the programme was interesting but for the terrible experience I had when breaking on the last day.

I ate boiled beef. I was enticed by the aroma and it was as if I had never taken meat before in my life. I requested for the hot meat, ate it (I felt I had to exercise my teeth), and after a while, I swallowed it. I then flushed it down with cold water. To me, that was enjoyable, especially after missing beef for good seven days!

But I was wrong. Not long after that, I felt a terrible pain that kept me rolling on the bed. I could no longer stand straight. When the bed was no longer comfortable, I moved to the mat on the floor. This continued for hours.

Thank God I did not complicate the case by taking any drug or eating any other thing again. The pain continued for how long I don't know and cannot remember, but I was sure not earlier than when the meat was finally digested. It was only after then I could stand up on my own.

## EXPERIENCE: THE TEACHER

Over the years, I have seen people going through the same hard lesson because no one taught them. You don't have to pass through the same pain. Experience is the best teacher. Take caution. This is why you are now reading this book to help you take caution and not because i want you to know we have done much fasting. Please make sure you don't experience mistakes of breaking a long fast wrongly. We love you.

My husband during his first 40 days had a bloating experience after he drank yoghurt four days after breaking. It was a terrible experience. He had to go on another 3 days fast, drinking only water and with serious prayers, before he was relieved.

I tell you, it is not good to break your fast wrongly. If anything goes wrong or you want to prevent such an occurrence, please ask for counselling from those who have practical experience in long fasting or read this book thoroughly. You could also buy this book and give to someone as a gift. There are lots of books on fasting but most books will not explain the practical aspects like this.

You may find that your body will be shaking as if all the food in your kitchen should just find their way into your stomach. Please take caution. Breaking a fourteen day fast will take you about four to five days or sometimes, half of the period of fasting, before you can return to your normal feeding style.

Women are more careful when it comes to food intake than men. So, wives of church leaders or pastors who may be on long fasts should be concerned about the breaking of their husband. Monitor all what he eats.

If there is any problem while breaking, it is advisable to go I tell you, it is not good to break your fast wrongly . . . please ask for counselling from those who have practical experience in long fasting or read this book thoroughly. back into fasting. This will help correct any wrong food you must have injected into your system.

> I TELL YOU, IT IS NOT GOOD TO BREAK YOUR FAST WRONGLY. PLEASE ASK FOR COUNSELLING FROM THOSE WHO HAVE PRACTICAL EXPERIENCE IN LONG FASTING OR READ THIS BOOK THOROUGHLY.

Just like in other types of fasting, make sure that you are always in the attitude of prayer. Your expectation should be high. Expect miracles. Keep your confession positive as anything you say will either strengthen your faith or destroy it. Read your Bible. Attend fellowship every time. Make sure you keep building up yourself. Do not relax. Watch your reading and make sure that the Word of God is constantly kept in your heart.

As a man of God, if you are a deliverance minister, handling tough cases will be easier. You have better results. Some levels of spiritual gifts will start to manifest in your life and ministry. If you had certain gifts before that have ceased to manifest, they will be stirred up. If you do all these things, you will have tremendous results. If your own fasting is for deliverance, then you will be delivered.

Operating in spiritual authority after ten or fourteen-day fast will give higher results, more than the seven days fasting. In addition, certain manifestations like healing the deaf and dumb, breaking the control of lower ranking territorial demons, casting out devils and gifts of faith can become noticeable after fourteen days.

# CHAPTER SEVEN

# HOW TO FAST FOR
# 21–40 DAYS

It takes a purposeful man to pray when fasting. The reason is that at a certain stage, prayer becomes a difficult task. Not because you are lazy, but because you do not have the strength to pray as expected. Prayer is one of the most difficult spiritual exercises and when combined with fasting, it takes only the determined man to pray.

When you are on any long fast, make sure you are praying with different prayer groups like the prayer warriors, the youth fellowship, the family forum, the workers unit, the ministers, and your own family for at least 3 to 6 hours daily. It does not disturb your fasting. It will only help you to pray and also throw challenges to those you are praying with.

Some of them may however sound discouraging to you when they see you squeezing your face because of hunger. So do not give room to any pity.

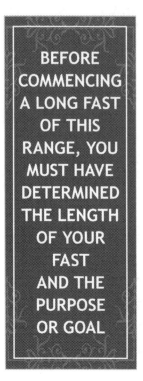

**BEFORE COMMENCING A LONG FAST OF THIS RANGE, YOU MUST HAVE DETERMINED THE LENGTH OF YOUR FAST AND THE PURPOSE OR GOAL**

Some people try to apply what the Bible says in Matthew 6:13, that you should not let your right hand know what your left hand is doing when you are fasting. But these people are the members of your church, family and friends. You are all one in Christ. They can know what you are doing and be encouraged to do likewise. Also, when they are praying with you, you will have the encouragement and the energy to pray.

There will be times when you will need to be quiet and alone. When you do this for 3 days, then you will call back to them again to have meetings with them and pray together.

As a pastor or General Overseer, it is advisable that you make a maximum use of this time by calling on your members, family by family, unit by unit and those that have special cases, to pray with them. This will be a blessing to them as well as to the church in general.

Before commencing a long fast of this range, you must have determined the length of your fast and the purpose or goal. Spend a lot of time meditating, and eat very light food before proceeding. Vegetables and fruits should replace the daily food some days before the fast starts.

When preparing for long fasts, you may need to treat yourself for malaria. This is due to the nature of our environment in Africa where mosquitoes easily transmit malaria disease which causes fever. Another area you may need treatment is if you are the type that eats too much of sugary things. Try and give your bowel some treatment. You can use 'agbo-jedi,' a herbal juice made from some of the leaves and herbs around. Beware not to buy this from the local fetish shops. You can make the combination yourself.

From the first day, start to drink water very well. On the 2nd and 3rd days, continue to drink water. Conserve your strength by getting involved in only those things that are extremely important.

During the first three days, you will be confessing all your sins, the sins of your family, the sins of your parents, the sins of the church, the sins of the community, and the sins of the nation. Tell God to show you every hidden sin and ask for forgiveness in the Name of Jesus. After 3-4 days, you will ask God to cleanse you, remove every impurity and He will cleanse you because God only wants to anoint a holy vessel. Psalm 51, Isaiah 58.

This goes on until the 9th day. On the 10th days, appetite will go. If you have been eating in the dream, or there is any poison in your systems, after the 10th day, your body will begin to burn them out.

The colour of your urine will change to deep yellow and have a strong odour. The odour that comes from your mouth will be very offensive. If you gas, it will smell like burnt excreta. This will continue until the 14th day, which takes you to the stage of advanced cleansing.

From the 14th to the 17th days, you will be asking for the endowment of power, the power of the anointing and the power of the Holy Spirit. The power of the Holy Spirit is different from the Holy Spirit. The Holy Spirit is the third person of the God-Head. His power is the equipment you need to do His job. Acts 1:8 says: *"You shall receive power when the Holy Ghost comes upon you . . ."* *The power of the Holy Spirit is the 'dynamism' to function.*

Jesus was baptised of John the Baptist in the river Jordan and the Holy Spirit like a dove came upon Him before an audible voice came from heaven saying:

> *This is my beloved Son, in whom I am well pleased . . . Matt. 3:17*

The Bible says He was full of the Holy Spirit and He was led into the wilderness to fast for 40 days and 40 nights. Then He returned in the power of the Spirit. Luke 4:1&14.

With the power of the Holy Spirit, you can enter into the realm of the supernatural. You get things done the way the Shepherd of our soul will get it done. You become another 'Christ.' (The word means 'anointed.') You can walk on the 'sea' on any storm of life. You can bind Satan; you can do anything in the spirit realm which will be manifested in the physical.

On 18th and 19th days, your body may have serious pains as if you were beaten at all your joints, particularly if that is your first time of embarking on this type of fast. If you have that symptom, it is a sign that you must continue because there are some battles going on.

The body enjoys cleansing from certain chemical deposits in the body system during long fasts. If you eat too much of canned food, sodium benzoate, sugar and caffeine, these will be burnt out from the body between the 18th and 20th days.

Some thoughts may come to you that you don't need to fast this long, and that you are now punishing yourself for what has been paid for on the cross by Jesus Christ.

> And he said unto them, can you make the children of the bride chamber fast, while the bridegroom is with them? But the days will come when the bridegroom shall be taken away from them, and then shall they fast in those days." Luke 5:32-35.

Then every orange will become yellow, you will be perceiving all kinds of aroma of food, people are cooking around you. You will feel like eating every food you see. You will repeatedly have to fight the thought that: if not that I am fasting, I would have eaten", and the devil will tempt you to eat small, that you have tried. At this point, don't stop the fasting. Continue. By the time you wake up on this 21st day, you will have new strength. Your breath is like a baby's and because you are not eating, the smell from your mouth will not be too good. So brush your teeth regularly. You will not be able to sleep too long, you will not be able to pray loud, because you have no much strength, pray inside, pray in the Spirit, pray all manners of prayer and supplication, pray in the Holy Ghost.

Try all means to bath regularly. From the 7th day, you may not be able to drink ordinary water. It may be necessary for you to heat up the water a little for easy drinking. After some days, you will not be able to drink ordinary water again. So you will add some milk, make it light, like a teaspoon to a glass cup of water or squeeze a little lemon into the water.

You may vomit during fasting. That is deliverance. If you are a woman, your period may suddenly come, it is also deliverance.

You can add some drops of lime. This may make you feel hot sensations in your throat and also make you look more famished if used for a longer period. If that is too tough for you, add very light honey to the water to give it some taste. (Read 7 days and 14 days experience).

If you know that you can drink ordinary water, all these are not necessary. But if not, you are allowed to mix it. Mind you, if this mixture is too thick it will break your fasting. How will you know? Your body will be shaking and you will be feeling hungry, then you will know that you've broken your fast.

After 21 days, you can break the controlling power of a particular region or prince in your area through warfare. Before you can break the power controlling every region through warfare, you will have to get to 21 days in your fasting. Warfare and deliverance anointing becomes regular as from the fourteenth day.

On the 28th day, hunger will return. At this time, if you see white rice and stew, you will feel like eating it but that has become poison as you cannot eat such a thing again at that stage of your fasting. Many people do lose balance or strength considerably between the 28th day and the 36th day. To walk even becomes very difficult. Some will have to even crawl on their hands like small babies. It is only for a while; you will soon get over it all. You will not die. Fasting does not kill. In fact, it is eating any how at this time that kills.

On the 37th and 38th days, you will experience 'death.' Naturally, it will appear as if all your organs had died. But the Holy Spirit will come and raise your body. It is part of the phase of the power journey.

Jesus said in John 12:24:

> *Except a seed of corn fall down to the ground and dies, it abides alone, but when it dies, it will spring forth and bring more seeds.*

What does this scripture mean to you? You experience the fulfilment of this verse on the 37th and 38th day of the journey of 40 days. You are similar to a dead man and the Holy Ghost fully comes into you and gives you a new life – if your motives are right for this fasting. You experience uttermost humility; you see God bigger than anything;

deeper than anything. It is awesome! This is why Acts 15:16 promises you to bear fruits.

You will feel like stopping but you must continue because you have to complete it. You will try to take your bath even if your spouse has to bathe you (if you are married).

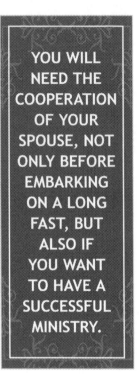

YOU WILL NEED THE COOPERATION OF YOUR SPOUSE, NOT ONLY BEFORE EMBARKING ON A LONG FAST, BUT ALSO IF YOU WANT TO HAVE A SUCCESSFUL MINISTRY.

Most people will need to sit down in the bathroom before they can bath. It is a very tough stage in fasting experience but it signals that you are making the last turn before the final destination. Try more.

On the 39th day, new strength will come. On the 40th day you will become stronger. At this time, you have to pray fervently. You will start to feel fulfilled as from the 38th day.

## DIVINE EQUIPMENT

All your experiences will start to come back to your memory with distinct understanding. Your vision and revelations become sharper. Divine equipment are released to you for the work of the ministry.

Equipment here means the spiritual tools for the work committed to your hands. Some can see themselves holding torchlight, driving a new car, using a caterpillar, operating a generator or wearing a new army uniform with stars attached on their shoulders.

My husband, during one of his forty-day fasts saw himself connecting electricity power stations and wearing different equipment. This is why he finds it easy to operate in most offices of the 5-fold ministry (Apostle, Pastor, Prophet, Evangelist and Teacher) – Eph. 4:11.

On the thirtieth days of my long fasts, I usually had burden for families for fruit of the womb. During one of such fasts, I had a revelation in which I saw an opener given to me specifically to open wombs. And on another fasting experience when I was doing forty days, praying for people in need of the fruit of the womb, I was given a key to operate a bulldozer. When I shared this encounter with my husband after my programme, he simply called me 'Barrenness Bulldozer,' which has become a reality in the testimonies that followed 'Operation Fruitfulness,' our regular programme for families believing God for the blessing of the fruits of the womb.

Weapons or equipment handed to you will be according to the assignment you are given, or as an answer to an area of ministry you believe God for.

## COOPERATION

An important advice here is that you will need the cooperation of your spouse, not only before embarking on a long fast, but also if you want to have a successful ministry. So carry him or her along.

*Two people are better than one, because they have a good reward for their labour. For if they fall, the one will lift up his fellow, but woe to him that stands alone when he falls for he has not another to help him up. Again, if two lie together, they have heat, but how can one be warm alone? And if one prevails against him, two shall withstand him and a threefold cord is not quickly broken. Ecclesiastes. 4:9-12*

# CHAPTER EIGHT

# BREAKING FASTS OF
# 21 DAYS AND ABOVE

When you are breaking the fast, you have to do so gradually. Some people say that fasting kills. Fasting does not kill. Nobody ever fasted and died. People who died in relation to fasting, died because they broke their fasts in wrong manners. Ignorance, not fasting, is the culprit here. This is why God inspired me to write this book and why it is very necessary for you to own a copy and give copies to your loved ones who will surely need the book in order to avoid making mistakes when breaking their fast.

On the 21st day your teeth may be strong, but your intestine will be closed like the intestine of a new born baby.

So, you can imagine the size or quantity of food or liquid the stomach of a baby can take at a time. You must break very slowly. You cannot eat anything like yam, rice, beans, roasted chicken, meat or any solid food. At this time they are like poison to your system, if you dare eat any of them.

Firstly, you will be taking diluted natural juice and light fish pepper soup. The longer the fast, the less the quantity of fish you can initially take to break the fast. While some fruits, like water melon are good, others like ripe pawpaw, banana, wine grapes, apple e.t.c could be dangerous because they can block the intestine, avoid all fruits with shafts during the first week of breaking 40 days.

You can take very ripe pawpaw only after one week of breaking. Swallowing pineapple shaft is not advisable until 7days after breaking your fast.

Anything you eat must be slowly taken and at calculated intervals. When you take something, wait for about 2-3 hours to see the reactions in your body system before taking another.

The principle of rightly breaking fasts is very important that anyone who is able to endure the rigour of waiting on the lord should be able to have real patience when it comes to breaking too. If you fast for 10 days, it will take you 5 days to break. If your fasting is for 20 days you will require another 10 days before you can complete the breaking to avoid any crisis. For 40 days, it will take 20 days to break. So you will be taking liquid food mostly when you start the breaking.

You may not have any problem going to the toilet especially if you stop eating heavy food 4 to 5 days before you start your fasting. Your faeces will be smooth. This is better than not to pass excreta at all. Between the third and the fifth day of breaking, expect some slight cramps and stomach upset when going to toilet. And until you have gone to toilet and back before we cannot say congratulations on your mountain top experience.

In case you break wrongly, don't go to the hospital. Go to a man of God who has experience in the area of fasting. The problem is not medically inclined. If what you eat during breakfast is causing you any problem, stop breaking and commence a soft or partial fasting immediately only on water.

As I earlier explained, when my husband did his first forty-day fast, he drank yoghourt on the fourth day, this resulted into his developing a bloated tummy and he became restless. He could not sleep, read, eat or even pray. His close prayer partner, a professor, now a minister of the gospel and presently the Assistant General Overseer (External), was advised to take him to the hospital.

As a scientist and a medical man, the professor was really worried so he came for my approval to take my husband to the hospital for medical treatment. I felt the problem was not medical. So after discussing it, my husband had to go on another 3 day fast with water only to correct the crisis. He could not even pray well. It was the Professor and I who had to undergo rigorous prayer sessions for him. Now, it cannot be as tough as that again. That was because it was the first experience. Thank God for His grace on the other experiences.

That was the only crisis throughout his breaking process, and by the time he was doing his second forty-day fast, there was no crisis at all because experience had taught us how to do it.

I am speaking from experience. Experience is the best teacher. You too can do the same kind of fasting. If you take the privilege of reading through this book, you too can make it through any fasting and prayer you might embark upon.

If you don't drink enough water when breaking, you will be feeling dizzy. If the water is too much, you will feel like vomiting. If you feel that way, go ahead and vomit. After this, you will be weak. As you break, you will be able to sleep more.

At this time, God will give you different inspirations. Some people at this point receive definite gifts represented in their revelations as various equipments. Some people may be given torches while some may receive generators.

Some people at this point receive definite gifts represented in their revelations as various equipments.

One of our men, who fasted for 40 days, shared an experience with me of how he saw himself attending a training session on telecommunication networks. He was connecting fibre cables to a telephone mast in a vision. When he finished his fast, his grace in the area of word of knowledge and wisdom changed dramatically. He finds it very easy to communicate the words of God, both written and spoken.

Another pastor in our ministry, who went on along fast, reportedly saw himself clad in an automobile engineer's uniform with spanners, pliers and screw drivers. He became an authority in manifesting some uncommon healing gifts. You may be given gadgets and artillery to manage.

One of my daughters in the Lord did forty-days and had the experience of oil being rubbed on her palms/hands. When she woke up, her hands were shaking rigorously. That was the healing gift from the Balm of Gilead.

Your guiding angel may be clad in big armour while some other may have an angel with machine gun. God has invested much in you now that He cannot allow you to be walking around unprotected like a 'common civilian.' This is because you have paid the price. It is not by might or by power but by the Holy Spirit. May God give you the grace. Amen.

Great success comes when great prices are paid. All the men of old who had made a difference in the history of the church in their own generation must have at one time or the other spent a particular time before the Lord in fasting and in prayers. Any careful study of the ministry of men of God in the past and in the present will reveal that outstanding results in terms of signs, wonders, miracles and healing followed them. Though there are many people today who teach that Christ has paid the price for all our pains and sorrows, and that by His sufferings, we are to enjoy divine healing. If Jesus, the Master of our souls, could spend as much as forty days and nights in fasting and prayers before confronting the task ahead of him, why should anyone now think less price will give a greater result? He himself told His disciples that "these kinds cannot be done, except by prayer and fasting."

Christ taught that He expects us to do greater works than He did. He also said He has committed much to our hands, meaning that much is expected from us in terms of sacrifices. He also said to the religious leaders of His time that the friends of the Bridegroom will certainly need to fast only when He is taken away from them. John 20:21, Luke 10:3.

The church of today has gone beyond the level of mere words or grammar. People want to see the living proof of the gospel we are proclaiming. The people who thronged after Christ in the Bible days were following Him not because of just His teachings but because He would not allow them to return the same way they came to Him.

The same way the church must be ready to see to the needs of the people if she really wants to remain dynamic. What a catalogue of messages cannot do, sign miracles will get done. How much quotations from the scripture will be required to penetrate the hearts of men in this generation? If only one blind person receives his sight in a meeting the gospel becomes easy to preach.

# CHAPTER NINE

# LONG DAILY FASTING

There are lots of elderly men of God today who can no longer embark upon long marathon fasts because of their age, yet they desire great results still in their ministry. To them, I advise long daily fasts. Once it becomes a regular practice, it will sustain the power of the anointing.

I remember a year when we were to do our annual marathon fast in the church (usually in January), my husband was unable to go on his usual 40 days fast because of the increase in both pastoral and evangelistic works. He had to do 120 days daily fast. During this time, I also supported him with just 100 days. We did not allow anything or give any excuse to avoid the fast because it is our covenant contact to the power the anointing. Despite the work load, the travelling around for crusades and television ministry, we still set aside time to fast.

These fasts and prayers brought a great explosion in the ministry that year. When a man keeps his connection to his source of power intact, there is no way the usual will not be manifested through him. There is no short cut to walking in the power of the anointing.

People will naturally go where there are results. Everyone wants the best option to a successful and happy life. If you want people to come thronging to your church, start to fast and pray on a regular basis and on appointment with God. If you want to start witnessing the unusual like hunch backs disappearing, the lame walking, the blind seeing, the dumb speaking (as experienced in our ministry), then get connected to the source of power through fasting and prayers.

Ministry work is not for the lazy minds. It is a real soldier's job; very demanding. You will need to give all you can physically, morally and spiritually. When you play your simple part, God will definitely play His own great role. He wants to upgrade you from your current position to a place of more results, but that means more commitments to prayers and fasting.

There are special tools in heaven waiting to be collected. The work we are doing now demands that we should always use new instruments. If there are new demonic invasions like HIV/AIDS, SARS and other deadly afflictions, then servants of God must be ready to face the challenge by always receiving new instruments of warfare from heaven through regular fasting and prayers.

Thanks to God that there is room for improvement in the ministry. Maybe the last time you fasted, it was just three days during which you saw yourself riding on a bicycle; that is just a level of anointing. If you can get a step further by doing 7 days or 10 days, you may receive the experience of riding on a motorcycle. You cannot expect a man on a bicycle and another one on a motorcycle to be travelling at the same speed. Please, increase your anointing and hence, your spiritual power to perform by increasing your days of fasting, either your daily fasting and prayers or your marathon fasting and prayers. As much and quickly as possible, move up daily fasting and prayers to marathon. The Lord will strengthen you to do so in Jesus' Name. Amen.

Spiritual power backed with fasting and prayers for a man who is rooted in the Word of God is explosive. It cannot all go in vain. Just give it a right atmosphere after which you begin to see and experience outstanding manifestations.

At this point I would love you to read the testimony of a man of God who read this book and later did a forty-day fast based on the principles enumerated in this book. I am sure this will encourage you.

# TESTIMONIAL
## By Pastor Olaleka Israel

I bought the first edition of this book in 2004. I read it and didn't really make much of it. The reason was that I wasn't interested in having the kind of long fasts prescribed there.

I 2010, I met Prophet Ayorinde in South Africa where I was involved in ministry. He looked at me and said, "Man of God, I have a word for you, but I am busy now, so if you'd be my Personal Assistance for today, I will have time to talk to you."

I was delighted at this. The prophet was a man I had been trying to get close to, and God was giving me this opportunity to meet him 'free of charge.' So I abandoned all I planned to do and followed him. I was with him in the car on his was to Pretoria from Johannesburg when he spoke to me. "Man of God, the Lord gave you an assignment several years ago and you refused."

I knew what he meant. The Lord had told me to start a church in Lagos, Nigeria in 2009, but because I did not like Lagos, I didn't commit myself to it. I explained my frustrations to the Prophet. I told him I had left my church in Lagos since two month to that time. "You left a church in Nigeria for two months!" he exclaimed. "Yes sir," I answered. I then added, "Miracles have ceased in Nigeria. My church is not growing. When I travel and minister, I see miracles: blind eyes opening, deaf hearing and even cancers healed. But in Nigeria, nothing!"

Then the discussion got to the topic of fasting. I told the prophet that I used to fast for five days in a month. But I had stopped. The reason, I told him, was that I fasted to the point where my intestines twisted. I was rushed to the hospital and had to receive treatment for months. So I concluded that I was done with fasts, especially long ones.

My negative experience with fasting was compounded by the minister friends that surrounded me at this time. They didn't fast, and they condemned fasting. They mocked me when I fasted and all these contributed to my stopping to fast altogether.

But the prophet Ayorinde spoke the word that changed my life. "Fasting is not the problem, but breaking the fast wrongly." He told me that I had been ignorantly hurting myself and missing out on the blessing of fasting because of the wrong way I broke my fasts. He enumerated some principles on fasting and breaking of fasts, I came to realise that I broke virtually all the rules. He encouraged me and told me to do it right the next time. Then he gave me some prophetic words concerning my ministry.

I had been praying about the state of the ministry at this time. Then God spoke to me to pay the ultimate price. What do you mean Lord, the Ultimate Price? He spoke to me definitely to fast for forty days without food, the type called forty-day marathon fast.

I went to Nigeria and dug out the book Anointing Through Fasting. I read through it, this time with a greater level of seriousness and I began to prepare myself for the fast. In 2011, I fasted for 60 days daily. During this time, our

Lagos Church picked up. In 2012, I told my wife we were still crawling, and that ministry was meant to be more than this. She supported me in all I planned to.

Since then I have done a series of 21-day 'dry' fasts.' One thing I quickly noticed was that my ministry took another turn for the better. I was delighted that this thing worked like this, so I went for the forty-day fast. This January I completed my second forty-day fast and I really enjoyed it.

This book gave me all I needed to know about fasting.

In fact, I did not experience many of the discomforts to be anticipated during such long fast. I climbed the stairs, fetched my water and did house chores throughout by the grace of God.

I learnt the following by experience: One, fasting doesn't kill, but breaking it wrongly causes damage. Two, fasting opens you up to divine encounters. I had numerous visitations during and after the fast. Three: fasting breaks yokes of stagnation. My ministry moved forward when I paid the price of total fasts. Four, Instructions are the key to success in any endeavour. The instruction I received through reading this book saved me from any damage and also made it so easy for me to fast successfully. Five: Fasting renews and reinvigorates. I am in my mid-fifties now and just concluded my second forty day fast. It has so much refreshed me that I even look younger.

I encourage every minister and anyone who wishes to be used of God to get copies of this book, study it and give to others.

# CHAPTER TEN

## CRUCIAL MATTERS ABOUT FASTING

𝔉asting and prayers are not enough to get you connected to God's power. He is no respecter of persons. He is a holy God and He expects nothing short of holiness from you, no matter the level of your fasting. Righteousness must be your watchword daily. The marathon fasting David did to save the life of the child born out of his illicit affairs with Bathsheba could not pay for his promiscuity. 2 Samuel 12: 16-19.

Another vital thing you need to take care of is your character. Fasting and prayers will bring the anointing. It is only holiness that will pre- serve it. What determines your profitability with the anointing is your character. When you are good and trustworthy, people will come to you. The reflection of the fruit of the Spirit in your life is a proof of the genuinety of the anointing on you.

# DON'T TAKE GOD FOR GRANTED

Avoid familiarity with God and the man of God. Fasting is not a convenient exercise. You are the only one who knows what you seek. Most great men of God had paid the price of the anointing at one time or the other. Your own case cannot be different. It demands some sacrifice, nothing good comes cheap. Anointing is costly.

**WARNING:**

There had been cases of people who are renowned sinners, drunkards, liars, fornicators, oh yes, people can do long fasts and they often come back with evil spirits or get attacked in the process. Their words are full of lies and doom. This is why you must check your motives and the type of life you live. Some have returned from long fasts and fallen into damnable errors of their lives. You cannot fast with a right spirit and motive and come down with errors. If your spirit is right in fasting, Psalm 32:8 comes into your life. Choose you therefore this day the servant of whom you want to be. If it be Christ, then get saved.

**YOU CANNOT FAST WITH A RIGHT SPIRIT AND MOTIVE AND COME DOWN WITH ERRORS**

Confess your sins, repent of them, live a holy life, stay away from sin so that when you fast, you have a better result.

Prayer and fasting move you from the natural realm into the supernatural realm and that is the only place you can get supernatural revelation, authorisation and power from the Holy Spirit as Christians.

So a long fasting without adequate corresponding prayer and holiness may expose the spirit of a man to this danger.

If you want to give your life to the Lord Jesus Christ today so that your fast can become more impactful, then say this prayer after me:

**Lord Jesus, I love you. Today, I confess all my sins to you forgive all my sins and take away all bad habits from me. Come into my life and live in me. Write my name in the Book of Life and establish me in your word. Lord, please make your grace available for me to make impact in my generation. Help me to walk steadfastly with you. Thank you, Lord. Amen.**

**Revitalise the grace of fasting and prayers in me now and assist me to be relevant to the furtherance of the work you have committed into my hands. Lord, help me now and always. I love you, Jesus.**

# BENEFITS OF FASTING OTHER KEY POINTS

**Why do I need long fasting?**

1. **For Deliverance:** if you are given food to eat in your dreams or having sex with a known or unknown person, you need deliverance. The food given in the dream

does 3 major things sickness, blockage of success and depositing of a monitoring power in your body. Usually such deposits are in the tissues of the body. They are not what medical specialists can detect or find solution to. Therefore in order to be delivered from such deposits, you may fast to the level where the tissues of the body will start breaking down, and at such stage, the deposits are dealt with.

During fasting the body utilises reserved energies in the following sequence: within the first three days, all the glucose reserves in the body would have been utilised. The next targets of mobilization of the supply of glucose to the body are fats deposits. The breakdown of fat in the body may continue until the 7th to 10th day of fasting. As from the 10th day to 14th day of fasting, the body will now move to the breaking down of muscles (protein).

The longer the fasting the greater the break- down. The purpose of this breakdown of tissues is to supply glucose to vital organs of the body such as brain. As the tissues of the body are breaking down, the "enemy deposits" are broken down with it and may be flushed out of the body. Drinking a lot of water and prayers will help the flushing out debris in the body. This is the reason why a single 14 days or more fasting at a go is more powerful and effective than several seven or less days repeated fasting.

2.  **For body cleansing**: cleansing of your body makes you healthier and live longer.

3.  **For killing all the killers in the body before their operational days.**

4. It gets you closer to God

5. It helps to put you back in good shape.

6. It gets you directly in touch with the angel called favour.

7. It reveals to you secret of the past, present and future.

8. Fasting and prayer are a destiny changer, where negativity is changed to positivity.

9. Revelations become clearer.

10. Inspirations get sharper.

11. The stamina to pray increases.

12. Understanding the word of God is clearer.

13. It allows for self control and self discipline over food, sex e.t.c.

14. Spiritual gifts are sharper.

15. It makes you help your family in becoming victorious.

Fasting is a must for all ministers especially if involved in a power ministry like deliverance. A deliverance minister who finds it difficult to fast and pray is playing with danger. He will soon get cast out instead of him casting out the devil. Nothing strengthens the spiritual gifts more than a good time out with the Lord in fasting and prayers.

Some sensitive gifts like word of knowledge, word of wisdom, discerning of the spirit and healings will be more pronounced with marathon fasting. A minister who fasts regularly will be able to heal the sick after regular fasting and prayers.

Healing gifts become more operational after 7 days of marathon fasts and prayers.

Casting out demons become easy after 7-14 days of marathon fasting and prayers.

Working of miracles becomes easy after 21 days of marathon fasting and prayers.

Breaking the power of territorial spirits become easier after 21 days of marathon fasting and prayers.

Power over principality like Belial (insanity), becomes easy after 30 days of marathon fasting and prayers.

Raising the dead becomes approachable if led by the Spirit after 40 days of fasting and prayers.

Full anointing to work the works of God after 40 days of marathon fasting and prayers.

As a woman and a mother who has gone through marathon fasts, I can see some similarities in the way you will be feeling when fasting and that of a woman during the early stages of pregnancy. Such includes:

— Weakness of the body

— Dizziness

— Thick salivating

— Vomiting (at times)

— Restlessness (sometimes)

— Loss of appetite (sometimes)

— Slight headaches (sometimes)

— Hotness of the body (sometimes)

A few hours you are ok, other hours, you are not. These and lots more inconveniences accompany pregnancy but none will be remembered after the delivery of the baby by the mother. The joy of the new born baby will make the mother to forget all the pains and troubles. The same with fasting and prayers. You have most of the symptoms above and even more. The reason is because you are 'pregnant' with all your requests. Yes you are pregnant! By the time you deliver, with gifts and manifestations of the Spirit; you will be overwhelmed with joy just as when you are overwhelmed with joy each time you have your baby. Your baby here now is your miracle your answered prayers. Always remember (though) that all the glory must be returned unto God.

Peace like a baby, your closeness to God and His word, revelations of secrets, joy in the Holy Ghost, oh! It is the best experience! Congratulations!

# CONCLUSION

Any pastor or minister who operates in the power ministry, especially in the area of healing and deliverance must be able to fast and pray regularly in fact fasting and prayers should be a part of his regular lifestyle. Fasting subdues the flesh and gives the spirit the opportunity to operate. It also sharpens ones prayer life. As you fast and pray to seek God's face, God will begin to plant an authority in you, born out of intimacy with him, that the demons will recognize and fear and take to their heels.

The only way to obtain and retain spiritual power (anointing) is to pay the price of fasting and prayer. Some ministers believe and often desire this anointing by impartation from a man of God who is carrying this anointing. In a way, anointing may be imparted but it keeps you running around to get who should impact you, why not pay the price and get the impact with it. it is more permanent. Jesus gave power to his disciples to go and preach the kingdom of God and to heal all manner of diseases and sickness. They were successful in doing that (matt10:8 mark 6:7, Luke 9:1-2).

However, when they were on their own later, they could not drive out the demon in a boy brought to them by his father. (Matt 17:15-16, Mark 9:18, Luke 9:38-40). When the disciples asked the master later on why they could not drive out the demon, Jesus told them that "this kind goeth not out except by prayer and fasting." (Matt 17:21, mark 9;29). They got impacted, but when Jesus left 'physically' they still had to fast before they experience more of the anointing in the acts of the apostle.

The height of the spiritual powers one attains during a long fasting depends on how many long hours are spent on praying and how much of god's word is in you. Our father in the lord, Prophet (Dr) Samson Ayorinde, during the first forty days marathon fasting and prayer, prayed for seventeen hours to receive the anointing to heal the deaf and the dumb, but the power did not come. He had to go back on his knees for twenty seven hours before he could receive the anointing.

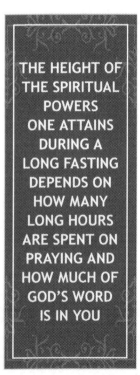

THE HEIGHT OF THE SPIRITUAL POWERS ONE ATTAINS DURING A LONG FASTING DEPENDS ON HOW MANY LONG HOURS ARE SPENT ON PRAYING AND HOW MUCH OF GOD'S WORD IS IN YOU

A middle-aged Evangelist came to our father in the lord after his forty days marathon fasting for prayers of impartation for power. During the fasting he dreamt or had some revelations that he acquired some machines, including a motorcycle and a generator but in the physical there was no manifestation. During a discussion it was discovered that he had never prayed at a stretch for five hours, during and after the fasting, to ask for the manifestations of such powers. He was counselled to go back and seek God's face for a longer hour of prayers before coming for impartation to establish his gifts.

It is my personal belief that a great revival is coming to this nation and the lord needs people to use for this revival. The revival cannot take place except we have people earnestly interceding for it with many hours of prayer. The servants of the lord who will be used directly for the revival must get themselves ready and like our lord Jesus Christ, be ready to pay the price of long fasting and prayers. If you are young and determined, you can be one of those the lord will raise up as one of the end time generals for the coming revival. This God-inspired book is therefore written to inspire, encourage and motivate you to rise up and be one of the people God will use for this great revival.

What i have done through this is to give you practical information on a personal experience on what you may expect during various kinds of fasting. It is my belief and prayer that as you diligently follow, the lord will increase your power to go through whatever level of fasting you decide to do and it will also be acceptable to the lord in Jesus' name. Amen.

# NOTES

# GET THESE OTHER BOOKS BY PROPHETESS AYORINDE

When Women Pray

Reversing the Curse

Woman You Are Beautiful

The Man Mordecai

Familiarity

To get Prophetess Ayorinde's Books, please visit the headquarters of World Evangelism Bible Church, 51-53, Ogudu, Ojota, Lagos.
Tel: 0803055534, 08033225513, 07025883013